'Ish

Sabrina —
You make me smile
w/ your goodness
+ joyful spirit!
Regina

'Ish

Getting the 'Ish Out in the Open

Regina Griffin

For Mommy,

You have been my greatest supporter,

biggest fan,

breath of life,

voice of wisdom,

and wings to fly.

I am because you are.

Thank you.

I love you.

What is 'Ish?

'Ish – A random, eclectic statement intended to provoke emotion – whether laughter, frustration, happiness or angst.

Statement creating a gust of thought.

A wanton expression or point of view.

'Ish #1

It's not your mama's macaroni and cheese if you used spaghetti noodles.

'Ish #2

If you can't tip at least 15%, get it to go.

'Ish #3

'Ish

Always faux. Never fur.

'Ish #4

If you do a #2 at a friend's house, pretend the door locked behind you by mistake, so no one goes in until the air clears.

'Ish #5

When you belch out loud in public, pretend it's a weird hiccup.

'Ish #6

If your co-pay is $20, shouldn't a co-person pay $10 of it?

'Ish #7

If your neighbor witnesses your car being repossessed, act like the tow driver works for AAA.

'Ish #8

' Buy leather shoes.
Wear cheap ones only on occasion,
in three hour intervals.

'Ish #9

Most relationships end like they begin. Make sure you can live by the standards you establish at the start.

'Ish #10

It's been eight days and you're still constipated. You don't need a stool softener. You need a specialist.

'Ish #11

Stop talking with green stuff in your teeth. I don't care that you just ate a salad.

You still have green stuff in your teeth.

'Ish #12

Fresh strawberries, whole milk and turbinado is not a smoothie. It's an overpriced milkshake.

Nice try though.

'Ish #13

Don't ask me how I'm doing! I said you have the wrong number.

'Ish #14

Eat at the bar instead of waiting an hour for a booth.

'Ish #15

Visit your grandparents' grave and take fresh flowers.

'Ish #16

Don't name your son Dick. That's mean!

'Ish #17

If you're considering artificial flowers for your wedding, call the county and get on the Justice of Peace's calendar.

'Ish #18

Instead of dining in, eat in your car and people watch.

'Ish #19

If your diet soda has zero calories, zero sugar and zero fat, what the hell are you drinking?

'Ish #20

Butter. Never margarine.

'Ish #21

Stop saying the only meat you eat is chicken. *It's still meat.*

'Ish #22

It's not a bagel. It's a fat yeast roll with a big hole in the middle.

'Ish #23

Give the homeless guy at the stop sign five bucks, even though his sign claims he'll *"work for food"*.

'Ish #24

The difference between a good and great tip is only about $3.

'Ish #25

Count the stars in the night sky, then close your eyes and make a wish on your favorite one.

'Ish #26

'Let your car sunroof back in the dead of the winter and blast the heat on the inside.

'Ish #27

Support a worthy cause with your time... *and money.*

'Ish #28

Give your child a name with meaning.

'Ish #29

Save $10 a week for your child's future. If you don't have one, save for another child in need.

'Ish #30

Buy at least two pieces of real estate in your lifetime - one for your personal residence, and the other as an investment for retirement.

'Ish #31

Utilize the laws of attraction to battle depression. Command that things already are what you would have them to be.

'Ish #32

'Buy flowers from a florist,

not a grocery store.

'Ish #33

Start a nonprofit. It's the ultimate way of supporting a cause dear to your heart.

'Ish #34

Once a month, spend a whole Sunday in bed . . . *watching old movies.*

'Ish #35

Date casually. Have sex cautiously.

'Ish #36

If a funny odor keeps following you, you might want to do a body cavity check.

'Ish #37

Kiss with your eyes closed.

'Ish #38

Put a down payment on a house,

instead of financing a wedding.

'Ish #39

'Forgiveness is for you,

not the offender.

'Ish #40

Speak loudly to use your voice as a barrier, *when you pass gas in a group of people.*

'Ish #41

Never refer to yourself as a victim. If you're still living,

you're a survivor!

'Ish #42

See two Broadway plays every year.

'Ish #43

When getting up from an embarrassing fall, keep saying,

"I'm okay, I'm okay,"

to deflect attention.

'Ish #44

Create a legacy to leave for your children, *even if it's just a lemonade stand.*

'Ish #45

Love yourself more than anything or anyone else.

It's the best suicide insurance policy.

'Ish #46

Maturity is characterized by your state of mind, *not your age.*

'Ish #47

Never forget your sweetheart's birthday, favorite cake or color.

'Ish #48

In your lifetime, walk a mile on a beautiful, sandy beach...
in another country.

'Ish #49

Drink champagne with your turkey sandwich.

'Ish #50

Never use salt at the table.

'Ish #51

Always anticipate a toiletry avalanche when you open your date's medicine cabinet.

Open with caution.

'Ish #52

Pass on the $5 haircut.

You get what you pay for.

'Ish #53

Have a facial at least twice a year.

'Ish #54

Wear your fine jewelry and best watch *with a t-shirt and jeans.*

'Ish #55

Make love with the lights on.

'Ish #56

Unless you're looking for a personal skycap, never make your new lover carry the *emotional baggage* left by your old lover.

'Ish #57

Do today, all that you should have done yesterday and may not have the chance to do tomorrow.

'Ish #58

Speech is silver, but silence is golden. See how long you can listen in a conversation before speaking.

'Ish #59

'Hold hands with your sweetheart . . . in bed . . .

under the covers.

'Ish #60

Use kindness to make a difference in the life of every stranger you encounter.

'Ish #61

Say I love you to someone today.

'Ish #62

Respect and treat the homeless like the rich.

'Ish #63

Never go more than a day without settling a dispute with a loved one.

'Ish #64

Wipe until the tissue is clean.

'Ish #65

Know when you have enough and give the excess to the less fortunate.

'Ish #66

Learn to swim.

'Ish #67

Stop and breathe. Seriously! Take a deep breath right now.

'Ish #68

Give in abundance, even in your lack.

'Ish #69

Relish a sun rising and setting,

at least once a week.

'Ish #70

In relationships, concentrate on memories and quality,

not titles or quantity.

'Ish #71

Do all the things people tell you are impossible.

'Ish #72

Always remove the comforter and decorative pillows from hotel beds.

'Ish #73

Worship a power higher than you.

'Ish #74

Wait 24 hours before making major decisions.

'Ish #75

Call instead of texting.

'Ish #76

In the winter, put your PJs and bath towel in the dryer for five minutes, before getting out the shower. *Warm and yummy!*

'Ish #77

Spend this weekend in a lavish hotel in the city. Relax, order room service and double tip the server.

'Ish #78

Never buy juice from a concentrate.

'Ish #79

Send a letter by snail mail instead of email.

'Ish #80

'Sneeze in a napkin.
Cough in your sleeve.

'Ish #81

Pray . . . everyday . . .

at least once.

'Ish #82

Turn off your cell phone after 8 pm.

'Ish #83

Brush your teeth before morning sex.

'Ish #84

Eat breakfast in bed, without utensils, while watching TV

– with the radio playing in the background.

'Ish #85

Find the teacher who made a difference in your life and thank him or her.

'Ish #86

Get a physical and have your teeth cleaned every year around your birthday.

'Ish #87

Buy two-ply toilet paper and use baby wipes afterwards.

'Ish #88

Get extra butter on your popcorn and add jalapenos.

'Ish #89

Drink green tea with honey,

instead of coffee with sugar.

'Ish #90

Check your nostrils and eyes for crustation before getting out the car.

'Ish #91

When in doubt, pop a tic-tac.

'Ish #92

Make love then finish the argument.

'Ish #93

Only fly 1st class abroad.

'Ish #94

Spend the day in the park instead of doing housework.

'Ish #95

Follow your intuition.
You don't need proof.

'Ish #96

Excuse yourself from the dinner table to blow your nose, and don't use the restaurant napkin. That's gross!

'Ish #97

Give 90% to the world, but always save 10% of you . . . *just for you.*

'Ish #98

Work hard and travel the four corners of the world.

Rest when you die.

'Ish #99

Wear thongs. Visible panty lines (VPL) suck! *MEN, DO NOT ATTEMPT.*

'Ish #100

Don't wait for the perfect time to get married and have children.

There isn't one.

'Ish #101

When referring to your dreams always use the word "when" not "if".

'Ish #102

Perfection only exists in the mind. Be flexible.

'Ish #103

Dance until your feet hurt, the lights come on and you hear the last call for alcohol.

'Ish #104

Stop bitchin' about Valentine's Day being a commercial gimmick!

'Ish #105

Go skinny dipping on vacation.

'Ish #106

If you aren't already a member, join the mile high club the next time you fly.

'Ish #107

Floss your teeth after eating ribs.

'Ish #108

Never look at the price when choosing wine for special occasions.

'Ish #109

If MapQuest says make a right, go straight. You'll get there quicker.

'Ish #110

Never be further than an arm's length distance from a bottle of hand sanitizer.

'Ish #111

Give your sweetheart the last piece of your favorite dish.

'Ish #112

Trim your toes nails before making love.

'Ish #113

Stop complaining about gas prices if you drive a utility vehicle.

'Ish #114

Coincidences and luck don't exist,

only fate and blessings.

'Ish #115

Learn the difference between a hotel and motel. Hotels have room service and daily rates. Motels have blinking, neon lights with hourly rates.

'Ish #116

If you didn't brush your tongue, you didn't brush your teeth.

'Ish #117

Never spend the holidays alone.

'Ish #118

If you charged it,
you probably couldn't afford it.

'Ish #119

Try everything TWICE before deciding you don't like it.

'Ish #120

If you're a vegetarian who eats bacon, but only on Sundays at brunch . . . you're NOT a vegetarian.

'Ish #121

There's no such thing as a social smoker. You just smoke.

'Ish #122

Use tissue to make a toilet life raft when using public restrooms.

'Ish #123

Pump gas for a stranger.

'Ish #124

For an emotional jolt, watch The Godfather trilogy, followed by The Scarlet Letter and Bridges of Madison County.

'Ish #125

Smile and hug more than you frown and argue.

'Ish #126

Walk instead of riding. Your booty will thank you.

'Ish #127

Pay the toll for the next two people behind you.

'Ish #128

Eat frosted flakes with whole milk . . . *from a china bowl.*

'Ish #129

Take a hot, relaxing bubble bath and eat strawberries . . .

dipped in white chocolate.

'Ish #130

Skip the soda . . . have water . . .

or wine.

'Ish #131

If your butt starts itching in public, pat instead of scratching.

'Ish #132

When having heated discussions with your sweetheart, sit knee-to-knee, holding hands. The dispute won't last long.

'Ish #133

Drive your dream car. You only live once.

'Ish #134

Plant a tree in memory of someone you love.

'Ish #135

Remember the richness in the sound of your parents' voice.

'Ish #136

Stop blaming your squinting on the text size. *You need glasses.*

'Ish #137

Buy timeless music and play it loud.

'Ish #138

Go one week without Tweeting, Facebooking, texting or emailing.

'Ish #139

Catch a morning flight to New York, have dinner, see a show and return home on the last flight out.

'Ish #140

Chronicle precious memories with pictures. You can never have too many.

'Ish #141

Use a handkerchief on gas pumps, ATMs and doorknobs.

'Ish #142

Keep a journal of your life, so your children's children will know you.

'Ish #143

Buy quality, durable underwear

and change daily.

'Ish #144

Back up your phone on your computer, *then back up your computer.*

'Ish #145

Use thank you, may I and please in every conversation.

'Ish #146

'Cry often to cleanse.
Laugh even more to heal.

'Ish #147

Never check the score during whoopi.

'Ish #148

Living in truth is the ultimate act of bravery.

'Ish #149

A vacuum cleaner is not a birthday gift. *It's a hint.*

'Ish #150

Never keep big secrets.

'Ish #151

Fear breeds shame, so fear nothing but God.

'Ish #152

Never send generic Christmas or birthday cards. *Personalize.*

'Ish #153

Artificial plants grow best in artificial light.

'Ish #154

Starting a sentence with, "honestly speaking . . ." is a perfect prelude to a lie.

'Ish #155

Buy at least one set of 800 thread count sheets for your master bed.

'Ish #156

Stop saying you don't snore.
You were asleep the whole time.

'Ish #157

Happiness is a gift you give yourself.

'Ish #158

Always give people credit for their intentions, not outcomes.

'Ish #159

You don't gain weight from eating after 8pm. You gain weight from eating TOO MUCH, after 8pm.

'Ish #160

Call your mama!

Made in the USA
Charleston, SC
27 December 2011